P9-DUP-660

Way of the Warrior

SAMURAI
Warlords of Japan

Arlan Dean

HIGH
interest
books

Children's Press®
A Division of Scholastic Inc.
New York / Toronto / London / Auckland / Sydney
Mexico City / New Delhi / Hong Kong
Danbury, Connecticut

Book Design: Michael DeLisio and Elana Davidian
Contributing Editor: Kevin Somers
Photo Credits: Cover © Bettmann/Corbis; p. 4 © Michael S. Yamashita/Corbis;
p. 7 © North Wind Picture Archives; p. 8 © Historical Picture Archive/Corbis;
pp. 11, 26 © Asian Art & Archaeology, Inc./Corbis; p. 12 © Private
Collection/Bridgeman Art Library; pp. 17, 18, 29 © SuperStock, Inc.; p. 21 illustration
by Kevin Somers; p. 23 © Bass Museum of Art/Corbis; p. 25 © Dallas and John
Heaton/Corbis; p. 30 © Werner Foreman/Corbis; p. 34 © Michael Maslan Historic
Photographs/Corbis; p. 35 © Maidstone Museum and Art Gallery, Kent, UK/Bridgeman
Art Library; pp. 36, 39 © Hulton/Archive/Getty Images; p. 41 © Private
Collection/Bonhams, London, UK/Bridgeman Art Library

Library of Congress Cataloging-in-Publication Data

Dean, Arlan.
    Samurai: Warlords of Japan / by Arlan Dean.
    p. cm. — (Way of the Warrior)
    Includes bibliographical references and index.
    ISBN 0-516-25119-8 (lib. bdg.) — ISBN 0-516-25088-4 (pbk.)
    1. Samurai—Juvenile literature. I. Title. II. Series.

DS827.S3D43 2005
952—dc22

                                                    2004003287

Copyright © 2005 by Rosen Book Works, Inc. All rights reserved.
Published in 2005 by Children's Press, an imprint of
Scholastic Library Publishing.
Published simultaneously in Canada.
Printed in the United States of America.

CHILDREN'S PRESS and associated logos are trademarks
and or registered trademarks of Scholastic Library Publishing.
SCHOLASTIC and associated logos are trademarks and or
registered trademarks of Scholastic Inc.

 2 3 4 5 6 7 8 9 10 R 14 13 12 11 10 09 08 07 06

Contents

INTRODUCTION

As the Sun sets in the west, bands of warriors on horses approach the outer walls of a castle. A shadowy figure advances from the group of riders. Riding high on his horse, the samurai shouts toward the castle, "I am Ashikaga Matatare Takatsuna, age seventeen. I am the son of Ashikaga no Taro Toshitsuna of Shimotsuke, descended from Tawara Todo Hidesato, the great warrior who gained great fame and reward for destroying Masakado. Here I stand to meet any on the side of the enemy who dare to face me!"

Suddenly, an arrow whistles by the head of the young samurai commander. Quickly, he takes aim with an arrow of his own. Its target is an enemy warrior, standing at a castle window. Sure of his great skill as an archer, Ashikaga draws back his bow. He locks in on his target and lets his arrow fly.

Yabusame is a ceremony in which archers on horseback perform the martial arts skills of thirteenth-century samurai. The archers shoot at three different targets as they race by them at full speed. *Yabusame* events are held throughout Japan.

With this single arrow tearing through the air, all the warriors begin to charge. The battle has begun.

The samurai were the legendary medieval warrior class of Japan. For more than one thousand years, they were the soldiers, peacekeepers, and rulers of Japan. The samurai lived exciting, violent, and often short lives. In times of war, they were fierce fighters, battling to the death in the service of their masters. In peacetime, they were gentlemen who appreciated poetry, philosophy, and finely crafted works of art. During many times in their history, samurai were landlords. Many men worked in their service, guarding or farming the samurai's prized lands.

Who were these unusual warriors who put bravery, honor, and loyalty above their own lives? For the answer to that question, let's take a closer look at the lives and times of the samurai.

The samurai rose to be the highest-ranking class of Japanese society. In feudal Japan, about 6 percent of the population were samurai.

CHAPTER ONE

Enter the Samurai

The use of the word samurai to describe the
professional warriors of Japan began sometime
between the ninth and eleventh centuries. In the
Japanese language the word "samurai" means
those who serve. Warriors had always existed in
Japan, but the soldiers who first earned the
name samurai were exceptional. Unlike many of
the part-time warriors who came before them,
the samurai usually did not work as farmers in
times of peace. The samurai was a full-time
warrior. He had only one job—to fight.

Samurai were usually from well-to-do
families. Since they did not have to work

Early samurai served as imperial guards for the emperor's court and
as members of security forces hired by lords throughout Japan.

to support themselves, they had more time to train as soldiers. Samurai were chosen to serve based on their skill at riding horses and using weapons. Young men chosen to be samurai were expected to do their duty and train in the arts of war. They were also expected to be ready for battle at any time.

Most early samurai banded together in clans. A clan is a large group of families. The samurai gave his loyalty to the clan leader. In return for loyal service, the leader loaned portions of his land to his samurai.

Land was important to the samurai because all wealth in Japan was based upon the production of rice. The clan leader received his land from a provincial governor. Each provincial governor was appointed to rule over a specific region of Japan. The provincial governor received his land from the imperial government, or government ruled by the emperor. The emperor ruled all of Japan.

As the Gempei War continued, the Minamoto slowly gained the upper hand. Fighting under the leadership of Minamoto Yoshitsune, the Minamoto were able to wear down the Taira army. The Minamoto drove the Taira off the mainland of Japan.

The final battle of the war was fought on the sea, off the coast of Japan. During this battle, the Minamoto destroyed the Taira fleet and completely wiped out the Taira army. By defeating the Taira, the Minamoto became the strongest clan in Japan. This allowed the Minamoto to break away from the imperial government and form its own government. Its leader was more powerful than the emperor. He was a samurai warrior, known as the shogun.

Rule by Shogun

By the late twelfth century, the shoguns took control of Japan. They ruled for nearly six hundred years. During the reign of the shogun, there was still an emperor in Japan. However, he was more of a symbol of Japanese tradition. The shogun held the real power.

The shogun now owned all of the land. Land was loaned by the shogun to powerful samurai known as *shugo*. The *shugo*, in turn, loaned land to less powerful samurai who served under them. As long as the shogun was strong enough to control the *shugo*, he could control all the samurai of Japan.

Between the twelfth and seventeenth centuries, samurai from different clans struggled to gain power over one another. If a samurai was strong enough to bring all clans under his control, he could claim the prized title of shogun. A shogun had to work hard to keep control over the *shugo* and their samurai.

A shogun would often keep family members of *shugo* as hostages. The threat of harm to his family would usually keep

In 1192, Minamoto Yoritomo became the first shogun to rise to power. This portrait of Yoritomo hangs in the National Museum in Tokyo, Japan.

a *shugo* from rebelling against the shogun. The shogun also forced many *shugo* to live at his capital city every other year. By doing so, the shogun could keep a close watch over the *shugo*. Through these forceful actions, the shogun kept his *shugo* in line. In the end, it was a shogun's intelligence and strength that allowed him to maintain power over the samurai clans.

CHAPTER TWO

Armed and Ready

In war, a samurai had many weapons to use. Battles usually began at a distance, so the first weapon the samurai needed was his bow. When gunpowder was introduced to Japan, a type of rifle called a harquebus began to be used for long-range warfare. Soon the harquebus replaced the bow and arrow.

When samurai needed to fight an opponent at close range, hand-to-hand combat would begin. Samurai used weapons such as spears, called *yari*, and the *naginata*, which was a long, curved blade attached to the end of a pole. The most famous of samurai weapons is the sword. The most recognized samurai

In the late fourteenth century, combat for the samurai changed. More of the fighting was done close up and therefore the sword became the samurai's weapon of choice.

sword is called the *katana*. The *katana* has become the most lasting symbol of the samurai.

Samurai Armor

Throughout their long history, samurai always wore some form of armor. Early samurai wore armor called *yoroi*. This armor was light and strong. It needed to be light so that the horse upon which the samurai rode would not have too much weight to carry.

Yoroi armor was made of small plates of iron bound together with cords of silk or leather. The plates were sewn into horizontal strips. These horizontal strips were then sewn together to make the entire suit of armor. *Yoroi* armor had a boxlike appearance. The armor was often painted black and the cords were usually brightly colored.

Elements of Samurai Armor

Kabuto
(helmet)

Sode
(shoulder plates)

Do
(breast guard)

Kote
(arm of armor)

Haidate
(thigh guard)

Sune-Ate
(shin guard)

Other pieces of armor completed the suit. Heavy shoulder plates called *sode* were worn on the upper arms. The rest of the arms were covered by long, cloth sleeves. These sleeves were covered with iron plates that were sewn in place. Sometimes, the right arm was left uncovered. This helped the samurai to easily use his bow. The helmet was a heavy metal bowl made of plates of iron joined together. Most helmets had a neck guard attached. Later styles of armor featured a more flexible design, which was necessary for samurai when they fought on foot with swords.

FIGHTING WORDS

Samurai who had no masters were called *ronin*. They often wandered throughout Japan, challenging other samurai to do battle. They viewed their skills as swordsmen as an important part of their spiritual growth.

The Philosophy of the Samurai

The samurai lived following a strict code of conduct. This code, which became known as Bushido, stressed the ideals of honor and duty. A samurai was expected to defend the honor of his clan. When necessary, he was also expected to give his life for the well-being of his master. The samurai's master was

This work of art by Utagawa Kunisada shows three *ronin* fighting. The scene is from an eleven-act play called *Chushingura*. The art dates back to about 1830.

usually a shogun or *shugo*. The failure to serve one's master with complete loyalty was considered a disgrace. To most samurai, disgrace was considered a worse fate than death. In many cases, a samurai would take his own life rather than live in disgrace.

In times of peace, samurai worked hard to understand their lives and their place in the world. The philosophy of Zen Buddhism helped them to do this. In fact, Zen Buddhism greatly affected the thought and culture of the samurai.

Zen Buddhism teaches spiritual growth through meditation. Meditation is a way of relaxing the mind and body with thought. Samurai who practiced Zen followed a strict

ZEN GARDENS

Some wealthy samurai used the ideas of Zen when decorating their homes and designing their gardens. Some Zen gardens did not have plants in them. These gardens were made of sand and large rocks. The sand was raked around the rocks.

Viewers could imagine the sand to be a river. The rocks could then be imagined as islands in the river's current. The sand could also be seen as the tops of clouds and the rocks as mountain peaks rising above.

physical and spiritual way of life. This practice led a samurai to enlightenment, or understanding of his own spirituality. Enlightenment allowed him to live without care or worry, even in times of great stress or pain.

The Rokuonji Temple, also called The Golden Pavilion, is a Zen Buddhist temple in Kyoto, Japan. It was built in 1397.

CHAPTER THREE

Warriors in Action

The history of the samurai is one of great battles and ongoing warfare. Samurai fought battles for the masters they served. The samurai were completely loyal to their masters. In return for their loyalty, they demanded to be rewarded for such success. The most common reward for success in battle was the donation of land by the lord to the samurai. Failure by the lord to reward samurai success was dangerous. A samurai who was not rewarded properly might bear a grudge against his lord.

Battles were fought for a number of different reasons. Some battles were waged against rebel samurai who fought against the

The samurai were so valued for their honor and loyalty that they became one of the most popular subjects for generations of Japanese artists.

FIGHTING WORDS
The oldest sword on record in Japan was sent as a present to Queen Himeko from China in A.D. 240.

power of the emperor or shogun. Other battles were fought between samurai clans who wished to steal the lands of other clans.

It is commonly believed that the sword was always the main weapon of the samurai. However, the sword did not become the samurai's preferred weapon until the fourteenth century. Before that time, the bow and arrow was the samurai's weapon of choice. Early samurai fought mostly on horseback. They used their bows in battle, trying to strike down their enemies from a distance.

Before fighting hand-to-hand battles, samurai were careful to choose the worthiest opponents. Choosing and defeating their most worthy opponent added glory to a samurai's victory. In fact, throughout samurai history, the most complete proof of success in battle was the presentation of the head of the enemy to the master.

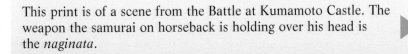

28

This print is of a scene from the Battle at Kumamoto Castle. The weapon the samurai on horseback is holding over his head is the *naginata*.

Castles

One important aspect of samurai warfare was the siege of an enemy castle. A siege is the surrounding of a place by an attacking army. The most powerful samurai built strong castles, which served as homes and fortresses to them, their families, and their men. When faced with an attack from a larger force, a samurai could retreat to the safety of his castle.

Starving an enemy was often the best weapon that an army had against a foe holed up in a fortress. It was a slow process to wait for an enemy to starve. Attacking samurai often tried to speed up the process by attempting direct attacks on a castle. Devices such as catapults and palisades were used during a siege. A catapult is a device that throws large stones. If aimed well, a large enough stone could break apart a wall of a castle and allow a direct attack. A palisade is

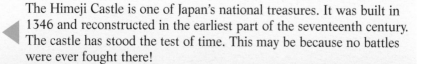

The Himeji Castle is one of Japan's national treasures. It was built in 1346 and reconstructed in the earliest part of the seventeenth century. The castle has stood the test of time. This may be because no battles were ever fought there!

31

a large, movable tower. An army would build the tower to the height of a castle wall. The tower was then pushed to the edge of the wall. The samurai could then climb up through the palisade and get into the castle.

If all else failed, an attacking army could use lies to draw its enemies out from a castle. For example, an attacking force would often offer a false peace treaty to an army in a castle. If the army came out of the castle to discuss the treaty, they would be attacked on the open field.

War of the Clans

Throughout Japan's history, there have been many wars and battles. One violent period, known as the Age of Warring States, lasted from 1467 to 1590. During this time, there was no strong imperial government. Local rulers, known as daimyo, fought one another for control of small areas of land.

In addition to samurai, there were also a large number of foot soldiers who fought. These soldiers were peasants and farmers.

A daimyo needed every man he could get for battle and was forced to train anyone who could fight.

The armor of this period was carefully crafted. It needed to be strong enough to resist the fire of a harquebus's shots and arrows. Each samurai wore a brightly colored banner on the back of his armor that was decorated with the badge of his master.

This photo from the 1890s shows a daimyo lording over his kneeling subject. This daimyo wears a black cap called an *eboshi*.

Forty-seven *Ronin*

Years of holding political power changed the samurai for the worse. By the late part of the seventeenth century, the codes of Bushido had been all but forgotten. In 1702, a shocking incident would remind Japan of the once-great ideals that Bushido stood for.

In 1700, Asano Naganori, the daimyo of Ako, lost his temper during an argument with Kira Yoshinaka. Kira was a powerful man in the court of the shogun. Asano drew his short sword and scratched the forehead of Kira. Asano was exiled and ordered to commit suicide. Forty-seven of Asano's samurai, now left without a master, swore to uphold their duties and avenge his death. For nearly two years, the samurai secretly plotted their attack on Kira's mansion. In December 1702, Oishi Yoshio, the chief of these *ronin*, led the raid on Kira's mansion. Oishi cut off the head of Kira Yoshinaka and placed it on Asano's grave. This was to show he fulfilled his duty to his master.

Forty-six of the forty-seven *ronin* survived the attack on Kira's mansion. They turned themselves in to the authorities and were ordered to commit suicide. Although these men broke the law, they acted in the manner of true samurai not seen in Japan for at least a century. The deaths of the forty-seven *ronin* made them a symbol of Bushido and returned the glory once lost to the name samurai.

This artwork by Utagawa Kuniyoshi was made around 1854. It shows the forty-seven *ronin* in battle.

CHAPTER FOUR

Exit the Samurai

Most of the nineteenth century was a time of crisis for the samurai. For hundreds of years, the samurai had ruled Japan in their traditional way. Then, in the early 1800s, the samurai way of life became threatened.

For decades, Japan and the samurai had tried to resist the influence of European nations. These nations, such as Holland and Portugal, worked hard to establish trade with Japan. Japan did not want such contact with the Europeans. The Japanese were afraid that European culture would affect their way of life. However, most European nations had greater military strength than Japan.

This Japanese print made around 1850 shows French diplomats riding horses in the port of Yokohoma, Japan. The ships sailing in the background fly the French flag.

Since Japan could not compete with the militaries of Western countries, the samurai government had a difficult decision to make. They needed to build the strength of their military to match that of the West. This meant that they had to accept some Western ideas and change their military systems. It was a strange position for the samurai government to be in. They had to become more like the West in order to resist Western influence.

As Japan industrialized, it became apparent that the samurai had no place in a modern society. They also had no place in Japan's new,

THE LAST SHOGUN

On January 3, 1868, the sixteen-year old Japanese emperor Mutsuhito of Japan held an early morning meeting. The emperor announced that shogun Tokugawa Keiki was to give up his position of power. Shogun Keiki was the last of the shoguns.

For more than six hundred years, the shoguns had ruled Japan. There had always been an emperor, but during the time of the shoguns the emperor had served only as a religious and a cultural leader. The shoguns had always held the real power of government. The emperor's announcement marked the end of the shogun era.

Mutsuhito, also known as Emperor Meiji, was only fifteen years old when he became emperor of Japan.

modern army. By the 1870s, the samurai had become outdated. Some samurai turned to new professions. Others drifted aimlessly, wandering the countryside unable to do the job they were trained to do.

A common belief is that the way of the samurai is found in death. Samurai had always served their masters, even if it meant they had to die for them. In the end, the samurai class had to die for the good of their greatest master. That master was modern Japan.

Although the days of the samurai are long past, their legend lives on. Their short and glorious lives still spark our imaginations. Their ideals of honor, duty, and discipline are ideals that we strive for in our own lives. To this day, the legacy of the samurai is important to the people of Japan.

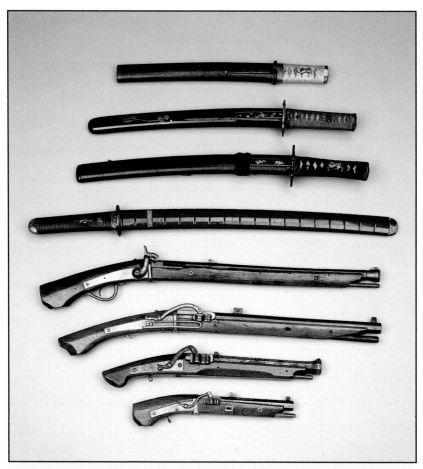

This nineteenth-century photograph shows both traditional Japanese swords and modern European guns. These weapons were made around the same time. This gives us an idea of the cultural changes that were going on in Japan.

New Words

avenge (uh-**venj**) to get revenge for

Bushido (bu-**shi**-doh) a code of behavior followed by samurai

clan (**klan**) a large group of families

daimyo (**dye**-mee-oh) powerful samurai who ruled over small areas of land

discipline (**diss**-uh-plin) control over the way you or other people behave

enlightenment (en-**lite**-uhn-ment) to reach a state of understanding

feudal (**fyoo**-duhl) the medieval system in which people were given land and protection by the landowner, and in return worked and fought for him

harquebus (**har**-kwi-buss) an early type of rifle introduced to the samurai by European traders

hostages (**hoss**-tij-ez) people taken and held prisoner as a way of demanding money or other conditions

legacy (**leg**-uh-see) something handed down from one generation to another

New Words

martial arts (**mar**-shuhl **artz**) styles of fighting that come mostly from the Far East; for example, judo or karate

medieval (mee-**dee**-vhul) to do with the Middle Ages, the period between approximately A.D. 500 and 1050

meditation (**med**-i-tay-shuhn) relaxing the mind and body through a regular program of mental exercise

samurai (**sam**-oo-rye) a Japanese warrior who lived in medieval times

shogun (**show**-gun) the title given to the military leader of Japan from the twelfth to the nineteenth centuries

siege (**seej**) the surrounding of a place such as a city or a castle to cut off supplies and then wait for those inside to surrender

Zen Buddhism (**zen boo**-diz-uhm) a religion based on the teachings of Buddha; Buddhists strive to let go of material things to gain spiritual knowledge

For Further Reading

Blumberg, Rhoda. *Commodore Perry in the Land of the Shogun*. New York: Harper Trophy, 2003.

Hall, Eleanor, J. *Life among the Samurai*. San Diego, CA: Lucent Books, 1999.

Kimmel, Eric, A. *Sword of the Samurai: Adventure Stories from Japan*. New York: Harper Trophy, 2000.

MacDonald, Fiona. *A Samurai Castle*. New York: Peter Bedrick Books, 1996.

West, Tracey. *Code of the Samurai*. New York: Scholastic, 2003.

Resources

Organizations

The Metropolitan Museum of Art
Arms and Armor (Permanent Exhibit)
1000 Fifth Avenue
New York, New York 10028-0198
(212) 535-7710
http://www.metmuseum.org/home.asp

Osaka Castle Museum
1-1 Osakajo, Chuo-ky, Osaka City
(06) 6941-3044
*http://www.tourism.city.osaka.jp/em/castle/
jozetu/*

Resources

Web Sites

Kids Web Japan
http://www.jinjapan.org/kidsweb/index.html
This site lets kids explore many aspects of
Japanese history and culture.

Thinkquest.org
http://www.thinkquest.org/library/site_sum.html
?lib_id=3800&team_id=coo1119
This site provides information on the castles
of Japan.

Japan's Way of the Warrior
http://www.samurai-archives.com/links.html
This site from *National Geographic* magazine
has wonderful photos, informative text, and even
an interactive siege of an ancient Japanese castle.

Women Warriors of Japan
http://www.koryubooks.com/Library/wwj1.html
This site provides a complete history of womens'
roles in Japanese martial arts from ancient times
to the present.

Index

Index

About the Author

Arlan Dean has written numerous books on a
wide variety of historical nonfiction subjects.
He currently works and lives in New York City.